# Stoicism and Mental Health

## BY BERTRAND RUSSELL

HALDEMAN-JULIUS PUBLICATIONS
GIRARD, KANSAS

# STOICISM AND MENTAL HEALTH

### (Written in 1928)

By means of modern psychology, many educational problems which were formerly tackled (very unsuccessfully) by sheer moral discipline are now solved by more indirect but also more scientific methods. There is, perhaps, a tendency, especially among the less well-informed devotees of psycho-analysis, to think that there is no longer any need of stoic self-command. I do not hold this view, and in the present essay I wish to consider some of the situations which make it necessary, and some of the methods by which it can be created in young people; also some of the dangers to be avoided in creating it.

Let us begin at once with the most difficult and most essential of the problems that call for stoicism: I mean, Death. There are various ways of attempting to cope with the fear of death. We may try to ignore it; we may never mention it, and always try to turn our thoughts in another direction when we find ourselves dwelling on it. This is the method of the butterfly people in Wells's *Time Machine*. Or we may adopt the exactly opposite course, and meditate continually concerning the brevity of human life, in the hope that familiarity will breed contempt; this was the course adopted by Charles V in his cloister after his abdication. There was a Fellow of a Cambridge College who even went so far as to sleep with his coffin in the room, and who used to go out on to the College lawns with a spade to cut worms in two, saying as he did so: "Yah! you haven't got me yet." There is a third course, which has been very widely adopted, and that is, to persuade oneself and others that death is not death, but the gateway to a new and better life. These three methods, mingled in varying proportions, cover most people's accommodations to the uncomfortable fact that we die.

To each of these methods, however, there are objections. The attempt to avoid thinking about an emotionally interesting subject, as the Freudians have pointed out in connection with sex, is sure to be unsuccessful, and to lead to various kinds of undesirable contortions. Now it may, of course, be possible, in the life of a child, to ward off knowledge of death, in any poignant form, throughout the earlier years. Whether this happens or not, is a matter of luck. If a parent or brother or sister dies, there is nothing to be done to prevent a child from acquiring an emotional awareness of death. Even if, by luck, the fact of death does not become vivid to a child in early years, it must do so sooner or later; and in those who are quite unprepared, there is likely to be a serious loss of balance when this occurs. We must therefore seek to establish some attitude towards death other than that of merely ignoring it.

The practice of brooding continually on death is at least equally harmful. It is a mistake to think too exclusively about any one subject, more particularly when our thinking cannot issue in action. We can, of course, act so as to postpone our own death, and within limits every normal person does so. But we cannot prevent ourselves from dying ultimately; this is, therefore, a profitless subject of meditation. Moreover, it tends to diminish a man's interest in other people and events, and it is only objective interests that can preserve mental health. Fear of death makes a man feel himself the slave of external forces, and from a slave mentality no good result can follow. If, by meditation, a man could genuinely cure himself of the fear of death, he would cease to meditate on the subject; so long as it absorbs his thoughts, that

3

proves that he has not ceased to fear it. This method, therefore, is no better than the other.

The belief that death is a gateway to a better life ought, logically, to prevent men from feeling any fear of death. Fortunately for the medical profession, it does not in fact have this effect, except in a few rare instances. One does not find that believers in a future life are less afraid of illness or more courageous in battle than those who think that death ends all. The late F. W. H. Myers used to tell how he asked a man at a dinner table what he thought would happen to him when he died. The man tried to ignore the question, but, on being pressed, replied: "Oh well, I suppose I shall inherit eternal bliss, but I wish you wouldn't talk about such unpleasant subjects." The reason for this apparent inconsistency is, of course, that religious belief, in most people, exists only in the region of conscious thought, and has not succeeded in modifying unconscious mechanisms. If the fear of death is to be coped with successfully, it must be by some method which affects behaviour as a whole, not only that part of behaviour that is commonly called conscious thought. In a few instances, religious belief can effect this, but not in the majority of mankind. Apart from behaviouristic reasons, there are two other sources of this failure: one is a certain doubt which persists in spite of fervent professions, and shows itself in the form of anger with sceptics; the other is the fact that believers in a future life tend to emphasize, rather than minimize, the horror that would attach to death if their beliefs were unfounded, and so to increase fear in those who do not feel absolute certainty.

What, then, shall we do with young people to adapt them to a world in which death exists? We have to achieve three objects, which are very difficult to combine. (1) We must give them no feeling that death is a subject about which we do not wish to speak or to encourage them to think. If we give them such a feeling, they will conclude that there is an interesting mystery, and will think all the more. On this point, the familiar modern position on sex education is applicable. (2) We must nevertheless so act as to prevent them, if we can, from thinking much or often on the matter of death; there is the same kind of objection to such absorption as to absorption in pornography, namely that it diminishes efficiency, prevents all-round development, and leads to conduct which is unsatisfactory both to the person concerned and to others. (3) We must not hope to create in anyone a satisfactory attitude on the subject of death by means of conscious thought alone; more particularly, no good is done by beliefs intended to show that death is less terrible than it otherwise would be, when (as is usual) such beliefs do not penetrate below the level of consciousness.

To give effect to these various objects, we shall have to adopt somewhat different methods according to the experience of the child or young person. If no one closely connected with the child dies, it is fairly easy to secure an acceptance of death as a common fact, of no great emotional interest. So long as death is abstract and impersonal, it should be mentioned in a matter-of-fact voice, not as something terrible. If the child asks, "Shall I die?" one should say, "Yes, but probably not for a long time." It is important to prevent any sense of mystery about death. It should be brought into the same category with the wearing out of toys. But it is certainly desirable, if possible, to make it seem very distant while children are young.

When someone of importance to the child dies, the matter is different. Suppose, for example, the child loses a brother. The parents are unhappy, and although they may not wish the child to know *how* unhappy they are, it is right and necessary that he should perceive *something* of what they suffer. Natural affection is of very great importance, and the child should feel that his elders feel it. Moreover, if, by superhuman efforts, they conceal their sorrow from the child, he may think: "They wouldn't mind if I died." Such a thought might start all kinds of morbid developments. Therefore, although the shock of such an occurrence is harmful when it occurs during late childhood (in early childhood it will not be felt much), yet, if it occurs, we must not minimize it too much. The subject must be neither avoided nor dwelt upon; what is possible without any too obvious intention, must be done to create fresh interests, and above all fresh affections. I think that very intense affection for some one individual, in a child, is not infrequently a mark of something amiss. Such affection may arise towards one parent if the other parent is unkind, or towards a teacher if both parents are unkind. It is generally a product of fear: the object of affection is the only person who gives a sense of safety. Affection of this kind, in childhood, is not wholesome. Where it exists the death of the person loved may shatter the child's life. Even if all seems well outwardly, every subsequent love will be filled with terror. Husband (or wife) and children will be plagued by undue solicitude, and will be thought heartless when they are merely living their own lives. A parent ought not, therefore, to feel pleased at being the object of this kind of affection. If the child has a generally friendly environment and is happy, he will, without much trouble, get over the pain of any one loss that may happen to him. The impulse to life and hope ought to be sufficient, provided the normal opportunities for growth and happiness exist.

During adolescence, however, there is need of something more positive in the way of an attitude towards death, if adult life is to be satisfactory. The adult should think little about death, either his own or that of people whom he loves, not because he deliberately turns his thoughts to other things, for that is a useless exercise which never really succeeds, but because of the multiplicity of his interests and activities. When he does think of death, it is best to think with a certain stoicism, deliberately and calmly, not attempting to minimize its importance, but feeling a certain pride in rising above it. The principle is the same as in the case of any other terror: resolute contemplation of the terrifying object is the only possible treatment. One must say to oneself: "Well, yes, that might happen, but what of it?" People achieve this in such a case as death in battle, because they are then firmly persuaded of the importance of the cause to which they have given their life, or the life of someone dear to them. Something of this way of feeling is desirable at all times. At all times, a man should feel that there are matters of importance for which he lives, and that his death, or the death of wife or child, does not put an end to all that interests him in the world. If this attitude is to be genuine and profound in adult life, it is necessary that, in adolescence, a youth should be fired with generous enthusiasms, and that he should build his life and career about them. Adolescence is the period of generosity, and it should be utilized for the formation of generous habits. This can be achieved by the influence of the father or of the teacher. In a better community, the mother would often be the one to do it, but as a rule, at present, the lives of women are such as to make their outlook too personal and not sufficiently intellectual for what I have in mind. For the same reason, adolescents (female as well as male) ought, as a rule, to have men among their teachers, until a new generation of women has grown up which is more impersonal in its interests.

The place of stoicism in life has, perhaps, been somewhat underestimated in recent times, particularly by progressive educationists. When misfortune threatens, there are two ways of dealing with the situation: we may try to avoid the misfortune, or we may decide that we will meet it with fortitude. The former method is admirable where it is available without cowardice; but the latter is necessary, sooner or later, for anyone who is not prepared to be the slave of fear. This attitude constitutes stoicism. The great difficulty, for an educator, is that the instilling of stoicism in the young affords an outlet for sadism. In the past, ideas of discipline were so fierce that education became a channel for impulses of cruelty. Is it possible to give the necessary minimum of discipline without developing a pleasure in making the

5

child suffer? Old-fashioned people will, of course, deny that they feel any such pleasure. Everyone knows the story of the boy whose father, while administering the cane, said: "My boy, this hurts me more than it does you"; to which the boy replied: "Then, father, will you let me do it to you instead?" Samuel Butler, in *The Way of all Flesh,* has depicted the sadistic pleasures of stern parents in a way which is convincing to any student of modern psychology. What, then, are we to do about it?

The fear of death is only one of many that are best dealt with by stoicism. There is the fear of poverty, the fear of physical pain, the fear of childbirth which is common among well-to-do women. All such fears are weakening and more or less contemptible. But if we take the line that people ought not to mind such things, we shall tend also to take the line that nothing need be done to mitigate evils. For a long time, it was thought that women ought not to have anaesthetics in childbirth; in Japan, this opinion persists to the present day. Male doctors held that anaesthetics would be harmful; there was no reason for this view, which was doubtless due to unconscious sadism. But the more the pains of childbirth have been mitigated, the less willing rich women have become to endure them: their courage had diminished faster than the need of it. Evidently there must be a balance. It is impossible to make the whole of life soft and pleasant, and therefore human beings must be capable of an attitude suitable to the unpleasant portions; but we must try to bring this about with as little encouragement to cruelty as possible.

Whoever has to deal with young children soon learns that too much sympathy is a mistake. Too little sympathy is, of course, a worse mistake, but in this, as in everything else, each extreme is bad. A child that invariably receives sympathy will continue to cry over every tiny mishap; the ordinary self-control of the average adult is only achieved through knowledge that no sympathy will be won by making a fuss. Children readily understand that an adult who is sometimes a little stern is best for them; their instinct tells them whether they are loved or not, and from those whom they feel to be affectionate they will put up with whatever strictness results from genuine desire for their proper development. Thus in theory the solution is simple: let educators be inspired by wise love, and they will do the right thing.. In fact, however, the matter is more complicated. Fatigue, vexation, worry, impatience, beset the parent or teacher, and it is dangerous to have an educational theory which allows the adult to vent these feelings upon the child for the sake of his ultimate welfare. Nevertheless, if the theory is true, it must be accepted, and the dangers must be brought before the consciousness of the parent or teacher, so that everything possible may be done to guard against them.

We can now sum up the conclusions suggested by the foregoing discussion. In regard to the painful hazards of life, knowledge of them, on the part of children, should be neither avoided nor obtruded; it should come when circumstances make it unavoidable. Painful things, when they have to be mentioned, should be treated truthfully and unemotionally, except when a death occurs in the family, in which case it would be unnatural to conceal sorrow. The adults should display in their own conduct a certain gay courage, which the young will unconsciously acquire from their example. In adolescence, large impersonal interests should be set before the young, and education should be so conducted as to give them the idea (by suggestion, not by explicit exhortation) of living for purposes outside themselves. They should be taught to endure misfortune, when it comes, by remembering that there are still things to live for; but they should not brood on possible misfortunes, even for the purpose of being prepared to meet them. Those whose business it is to deal with the young must keep a close watch upon themselves to see that they do not derive a sadistic pleasure from the necessary element of discipline in education; the motive for discipline must always be the development of character or intelligence.

For the intellect, also, requires discipline, without which accuracy will never be achieved. But the discipline of the intellect is a different topic, and lies outside the scope of this essay.

I have only one more word to say, and that is, that discipline is best when it springs from an inner impulse. In order that this may be possible, it is necessary that the child or adolescent should feel the ambition to achieve something difficult, and should be willing to make efforts to that end. Such ambition is usually suggested by some person in the environment; thus even self-discipline depends, in the end, upon an educational stimulus.

# MODERN HOMOGENEITY

## (Written in 1930)

The European traveller in America—at least if I may judge by myself—is struck by two peculiarities: first the extreme similarity of outlook in all parts of the United States (except the old South), and secondly the passionate desire of each locality to prove that it is peculiar and different from every other. The second of these is, of course, caused by the first. Every place wishes to have a reason for local pride, and therefore cherishes whatever is distinctive in the way of geography or history or tradition. The greater the uniformity that in fact exists, the more eager becomes the search for differences that may mitigate it. The old South is in fact quite unlike the rest of America, so unlike that one feels as if one had arrived in a different country. It is agricultural, aristocratic, and retrospective, whereas the rest of America is industrial, democratic, and prospective. When I say that America outside the old South is industrial, I am thinking even of those parts that are devoted almost wholly to agriculture, for the mentality of the American agriculturist is industrial. He uses much modern machinery; he is intimately dependent upon the railway and the telephone; he is very conscious of the distant markets to which his products are sent; he is in fact a capitalist who might just as well be in some other business. A peasant, as he exists in Europe and Asia, is practically unknown in the United States. This is an immense boon to America, and perhaps its most important superiority as compared to the Old World, for the peasant everywhere is cruel, avaricious, conservative, and inefficient. I have seen orange groves in Sicily and orange groves in California; the contrast represents a period of about two thousand years. Orange groves in Sicily are remote from trains and ships; the trees are old and gnarled and beautiful; the methods are those of classical antiquity. The men are ignorant and semi-savage, mongrel descendants of Roman slaves and Arab invaders; what they lack in intelligence towards trees they make up for by cruelty to animals. With moral degradation and economic incompetence goes an instinctive sense of beauty which is perpetually reminding one of Theocritus and the myth about the Garden of the Hesperides. In a Californian orange grove the Garden of the Hesperides seems very remote. The trees are all exactly alike, carefully tended and at the right distance apart. The oranges, it is true, are not all exactly of the same size, but careful machinery sorts them so that automatically all those in one box are exactly similar. They travel along with suitable things being done to them by suitable machines at suitable points until they enter a suitable refrigerator car in which they travel to a suitable market. The machine stamps the words "Sunkist" upon them, but otherwise there is nothing to suggest that nature has any part in their production. Even the climate is artificial, for when there would otherwise be frost, the orange grove is kept artificially warm by a pall of smoke. The men engaged in agriculture of this kind do not feel themselves, like the agriculturists of former times, the patient servants of natural forces; on the contrary, they feel themselves the masters, and able to bend natural forces to their will. There is there-fore not the same difference in America as in the Old World between the outlook of industrialists and that of agriculturists. The important part of the environment in America is the human part; by comparison the non-human part sinks into insignificance. I was constantly assured in Southern California that the climate turned people into lotus eaters, but I confess I saw no evidence of this. They seemed to me exactly like the people in Minneapolis or Winnipeg, although climate, scenery, and natural conditions were as different as possible in the two regions. When one considers the difference between a Norwegian and a Sicilian, and compares it with the lack of difference between a man from (say) North Dakota and a man from Southern California, one realizes the immense revolution in human affairs which has been brought about by man's becoming the master instead of the slave of his physical environment. Norway and Sicily both have ancient traditions; they had pre-Christian religions embodying men's reactions to the climate, and when Christianity came it inevitably took very different forms in the two countries. The Norwegian feared ice and snow; the Sicilian feared lava and earthquakes. Hell was invented in a southern climate; if it had been invented in Norway, it would have been cold. But neither in North Dakota nor in Southern California is Hell a climatic condition: in both it is a stringency on the money market. This illustrates the un-importance of climate in modern life.

America is a man-made world; moreover it is a world which man has made by means of machinery. I am thinking not only of the physical environment, but also and quite as much of thoughts and emotions. Consider a really stirring murder: the murderer, it is true, may be primi-tive in his methods, but those who spread the knowledge of his deed do so by means of all the latest resources of science. Not only in the great cities, but in lonely farms on the prairie and in mining camps in the Rockies, the radio disseminates all the latest information, so that half the topics of conversation on a given day are the same in every household throughout the country. As I was crossing the plains in the train, endeavouring not to hear a loud-speaker bellowing advertise-ments of soap, an old farmer came up to me with a beaming face and said, "Wherever you go nowadays you can't get away from civilization." Alas! How true! I was endeavouring to read Virginia Woolf, but the advertisements won the day.

Uniformity in the physical apparatus of life would be no grave matter, but uniformity in matters of thought and opinion is much more dangerous  It is, however, a quite inevitable result of modern in-ventions. Production is cheaper when it is unified and on a large scale than when it is divided into a number of small units. This applies quite as much to the production of opinions as to the production of pins. The principal sources of opinion in the present day are the schools, the Churches, the Press, the cinema, and the radio. The teaching in the elementary schools must inevitably become more and more standardized as more use is made of apparatus. It may, I think, be assumed that both the cinema and the radio will play a rapidly increasing part in school education in the near future. This will mean that the lessons will be produced at a centre and will be precisely the same wherever the material prepared at this centre is used. Some Churches, I am told, send out every week a model sermon to all the less educated of their clergy, who, if they are governed by the ordinary laws of human nature, are no doubt grateful for being saved the trouble of composing a sermon of their own. This model sermon, of course, deals with some burning topic of the moment, and aims at arousing a given mass emotion throughout the length and breadth of the land. The same thing applies in a higher degree to the Press, which receives everywhere the same telegraphic news and is syndicated on a large scale. Reviews of my books, I find, are, except in the best newspapers, verbally the same from New York to San Francisco, and from Maine to Texas, except that they become shorter as one travels from the north-east to the south-west.

Perhaps the greatest of all forces for uniformity in the modern world is the cinema, since its influence is not confined to America but penetrates to all parts of the world, except the Soviet Union, which, however, has its own different uniformity. The cinema embodies, broadly speaking, Hollywood's opinion of what is liked in the Middle West. Our emotions in regard to love and marriage, birth and death, are becoming standardized according to this recipe. To the young of all lands Hollywood represents the last word in modernity, displaying both the pleasures of the rich and the methods to be adopted for acquiring riches. I suppose the talkies will lead before long to the adoption of a universal language, which will be that of Hollywood.

It is not only among the comparatively ignorant that there is uniformity in America. The same thing applies, though in a slightly less degree, to culture. I visited book shops in every part of the country, and found everywhere the same best-sellers prominently displayed. So far as I could judge, the cultured ladies of America buy every year about a dozen books, the same dozen everywhere. To an author this is a very satisfactory state of affairs, provided he is one of the dozen. But it certainly does mark a differnce from Europe, where there are many books with small sales rather than a few with large sales.

It must not be supposed that the tendency towards uniformity is either wholly good or wholly bad. It has great advantages and also great disadvantages: its chief advantage is, of course, that it produces a population capable of peaceable co-operation; its great disadvantage is that it produces a population prone to persecution of minorities. This latter defect is probably temporary, since it may be assumed that before long there will be no minorities. A great deal depends, of course, on how the uniformity is achieved. Take, for example, what the schools do to southern Italians. Southern Italians have been distinguished throughout history for murder, graft, and aesthetic sensibility. The Public Schools effectively cure them of the last of these three, and to that extent assimilate them to the native American population, but in regard to the other two distinctive qualities, I gather that the success of the schools is less marked. This illustrates one of the dangers of uniformity as an aim: good qualities are easier to destroy than bad ones, and therefore uniformity is most easily achieved by lowering all standards. It is, of course, clear that a country with a large foreign population must endeavour, through its schools, to assimilate the children of immigrants, and therefore a certain degree of Americanization is inevitable. It is, however, unfortunate that such a large part of this process should be effected by means of a somewhat blatant nationalism. America is already the strongest country in the world, and its preponderance is continually increasing. This fact naturally inspires fear in Europe, and the fear is increased by everything suggesting militant nationalism. It may be the destiny of America to teach political good sense to Europe, but I am afraid that the pupil is sure to prove refractory.

With the tendency towards uniformity in America there goes, as it seems to me, a mistaken conception of democracy. It seems to be generally held in the United States that democracy requires all men to be alike, and that, if a man is in any way different from another, he is "setting himself up" as superior to that other. France is quite as democratic as America, and yet this idea does not exist in France. The doctor, the lawyer, the priest, the public official are all different types in France; each profession has its own traditions and its own standards, although it does not set up to be superior to other professions. In America all professional men are assimilated in type to the business man. It is as though one should decree that an orchestra should consist only of violins. There does not seem to be an adequate understanding of the fact that society should be a pattern or an organism, in which different organs play different parts. Imagine the eye and the ear quarrelling as to whether it is better to see or to hear, and deciding that each would do neither since neither could do both. This, it seems to me, would be democracy as understood in America. There is a strange envy of any kind of excellence which cannot be universal except, of course, in the sphere of athletics and sport, where aristocracy is enthusiastically acclaimed. It seems that the average American is more capable of humility in regard to his muscles than in regard to his brains; perhaps this is because his admiration for muscle is more profound and genuine than his admiration of brains. The flood of popular scientific books in America is inspired partly, though of course not wholly, by the unwillingness to admit that there is anything in science which only experts can understand. The idea that a special training may be necessary to understand, say, the theory of relativity, causes a sort of irritation, although nobody is irritated by the fact that a special training is necessary in order to be a first-rate football player.

Achieved eminence is perhaps more admired in America than in any other country, and yet the road to certain kinds of eminence is made very difficult for the young, because people are intolerant of any eccentricity or anything that could be called "setting one's self up," provided the person concerned is not already labelled "eminent." Consequently many of the finished types that are most admired are difficult to produce at home and have to be imported from Europe. This fact is bound up with standardization and uniformity. Exceptional merit, especially in artistic directions, is bound to meet with great obstacles in youth so long as everybody is expected to conform outwardly to a pattern set by the successful executive.

Standardization, though it may have disadvantages for the exceptional individual, probably increases the happiness of the average man, since he can utter his thoughts with a certainty that they will be like the thoughts of his hearer. Moreover it promotes national cohesion, and makes politics less bitter and violent than where more marked differences exist. I do not think it is possible to strike a balance of gains and losses, but I think the standardization which now exists in America is likely to exist throughout Europe as the world becomes more mechanized. Europeans, therefore, who find fault with America on this account should realize that they are finding fault with the future of their own countries, and are setting themselves against an inevitable and universal trend in civilization. Undoubtedly internationalism will become easier as the differences between nations diminish, and if once internationalism were established, social cohesion would become of enormous importance for preserving internal peace. There is a certain risk, which cannot be denied, of an immobility analogous to that of the late Roman Empire. But as against this, we may set the revolutionary forces of modern science and modern technique. Short of a universal intellectual decay, these forces, which are a new feature in the modern world, will make immobility impossible, and prevent that kind of stagnation which has overtaken great empires in the past. Arguments from history are dangerous to apply to the present and the future, because of the complete change that science has introduced. I see therefore no reason for undue pessimism, however standardization may offend the tastes of those who are unaccustomed to it.

## MEN *VERSUS* INSECTS

(Written in 1933)

Amid wars and rumours of wars, while "disarmament" proposals and non-aggression pacts threaten the human race with unprecedented disaster, another conflict, perhaps even more important, is receiving much less notice than it deserves—I mean the conflict between men and insects.

We are accustomed to being the Lords of Creation; we no longer have occasion, like the cave men, to fear lions and tigers, mammoths and wild boars. Except against each other, we feel ourselves safe. But while big animals no longer threaten our existence, it is otherwise with small animals. Once before in the history of life on this planet, large animals gave place to small ones. For many ages dinosaurs ranged unconcerned through swamp and forest, fearing nothing but each other, not doubting the absoluteness of their empire But they disappeared, to give place to tiny mammals—mice, small hedgehogs, miniature horses no bigger than rats, and such-like. Why the dinosaurs died out is not known, but it is supposed to be because they had minute brains and devoted themselves to the growth of weapons of offence in the shape of numerous horns. However that may be, it was not through their line that life developed.

The mammals, having become supreme, proceeded to grow big. But the biggest on land, the mammoth, is extinct, and the other large animals have grown rare, except man and those that he has domesticated. Man, by his intelligence, has succeeded in finding nourishment for a large population, in spite of his size. He is safe, except from the little creatures—the insects and the micro-organisms.

Insects have an initial advantage in their numbers. A small wood may easily contain as many ants as there are human beings in the whole world. They have another advantage in the fact that they eat our food before it is ripe for us. Many noxious insects' which used to live only in some one comparatively small region have been unintentionally transported by man to new environments where they have done immense damage. Travel and trade are useful to insects as well as to micro-organisms. Yellow fever formerly existed only in West Africa, but was carried to the Western hemisphere by the slave trade. Now, owing to the opening up of Africa, it is gradually travelling eastward across that continent. When it reaches the east coast it will become almost impossible to keep it out of India and China, where it may be expected to halve the population. Sleeping sickness is an even more deadly African disease which is gradually spreading.

Fortunately science has discovered ways by which insect pests can be kept under. Most of them are liable to parasites which kill so many that the survivors cease to be a serious problem, and entomologists are engaged in studying and breeding such parasites. Official reports of their activities are fascinating; they are full of such sentences as: "He proceeded to Brazil, at the request of the planters of Trinidad, to search for the natural enemies of the sugar-cane Froghopper." One would say that the sugar-cane Froghopper would have little chance in this contest. Unfortunately, so long as war continues, all scientific knowledge is double-edged. For example, Professor Fritz Haber, who has just died, invented a process for the fixation of nitrogen.. He intended it to increase the fertility of the soil, but the German Government used it for the manufacture of high explosives, and has recently exiled him for preferring manure to bombs. In the next great war, the scientists on either side will let loose pests on the crops of the other side, and it may prove scarcely possible to destroy the pests when peace comes. The more we know, the more harm we can do each other. If human beings, in their rage against each other, invoke the aid of insects and micro-organisms, as they certainly will do if there is another big war, it is by no means unlikely that the insects will remain the sole ultimate victors. Perhaps, from a cosmic point of view, this is not to be regretted; but as a human being I cannot help heaving a sigh over my own species.

# ON COMETS

If I were a comet, I should consider the men of our present age a degenerate breed.

In former times, the respect for comets was universal and profound. One of them foreshadowed the death of Caesar; another was regarded as indicating the approaching death of the Emperor Vespasian. He himself was a strong-minded man, and maintained that the comet must have some other significance, since it was hairy and he was bald; but there were few who shared this extreme of Rationalism. The Venerable Bede said that "comets portend revolutions of kingdoms, pestilence, war, winds, or heat." John Knox regarded comets as evidences of divine anger, and other Scottish Protestants thought them "a warning to the King to extirpate the Papists."

America, and especially New England, came in for a due share of cometary attention. In 1652 a comet appeared just at the moment when the eminent Mr. Cotton fell ill, and disappeared at his death. Only ten years later, the wicked inhabitants of Boston were warned by a new comet to abstain from "voluptuousness and abuse of the good creatures of God by licentiousness in drinking and fashions in apparel." Increase Mather, the eminent divine, considered that comets and eclipses had portended the deaths of Presidents of Harvard and Colonial Governors, and instructed his flock to pray to the Lord that he would not "take away stars and send comets to succeed them."

All this superstition was gradually dispelled by Halley's discovery that one comet, at least, went round the sun in an orderly ellipse, just like a sensible planet, and by Newton's proof that comets obey the law of gravitation. For some time, Professors in the more old-fashioned universities were forbidden to mention these discoveries, but in the long run the truth could not be concealed.

In our day, it is difficult to imagine a world in which everybody, high and low, educated and uneducated, was preoccupied with comets, and filled with terror whenever one appeared. Most of us have never seen a comet. I have seen two, but they were far less impressive than I had expected them to be. The cause of the change in our attitude is not merely Rationalism, but artificial lighting. In the streets of a modern city the night sky is invisible; in rural districts, we move in cars with bright headlights. We have blotted out the heavens and only a few scientists remain aware of stars and planets, meteorites and comets. The world of our daily life is more man-made than at any previous epoch. In this there is loss as well as gain: Man, in the security of his dominion, is becoming trivial, arrogant, and a little mad. But I do not think a comet would now produce the wholesome moral effect which it produced in Boston in 1662; a stronger medicine would now be needed.

# NOTES AND COMMENTS

## By E. Haldeman-Julius

*Reprinted from The American Freeman, Published at Girard, Kansas.*

## SOME LAST WORDS OF H. G. WELLS

Writing of "Babes in the Darkling Wood," H. G. Wells observed, "You can bring up one divinity after another to me and I can say definitely of each one, it is absolutely impossible to believe there can be any such God as this." How far from "God the Invisible King," H. G's. creation after World War I!

And again, "Men's education is still overshadowed by the tradition of monks, and women's education is still overshadowed by men's and ruled by spinsters." However a spinster, Ellen Wilkinson, who has just followed Wells to the grave, fought a noble battle for better education in Britain, and, thanks to Herbert Morrison, English school-children are now confronted by the legend, "The teacher may be wrong. Think for yourself."

❖ ❖ ❖

## LET'S BE OBJECTIVE ABOUT RUSSIA

If you are objective in your digestion of factual information, or, in other words, have not been unduly influenced by propaganda for or against Russia, you should make a point of reading William Mandel's new book, entitled "A Guide to the Soviet Union." The present writer, who prefers statistics to wishful thinking on any subject, has no deep love for totalitarian Communism, but while he has read many books, both pro and con, on the subject of Russia, he is willing to especially recommend this "Guide" of Mandel's.

One is astonished, not only about things which greatly impressed people like Wendell Willkie and Eric Johnston, but what has been accomplished culturally and medically by Russia in recent years. Although our American Medical Association has been continually damning socialized medicine, it is pretty dumb about the practice of medicine in the only country where socialized medicine is actually operating and doctors are all employes of the State. Have we cut our own national death-rate 45 percent for adults and 50 percent for children since 1913? True, Russia's death-rate is still somewhat higher than ours, but will it be higher after 10 or 15 more years?

It is also true that the man-hour of an American worker is still more productive in industry than the man-hour of a Russian, but while Russia increased man-hour productivity 12 percent per annum on an average during her five-year plans, we only increased ours 3.7 per annum during that boom period of 1922-1929, and 3 percent yearly, according to one recent calculator, during the last war. This difference, I suggest, is due to Russian overhead economic planning in contrast to our own "free enterprise" anarchy.

❖   ❖   ❖

## THE CHURCHILL LIBEL CASE

A London publisher once said that the British law of libel is that if you bring an action for libel you win it. We Americans sometimes forget that. So the fact that Winston Churchill didn't have to press the libel suit against Harper Brothers which attracted so much interest means less than the average American is inclined to think; especially if you remember the kind of jury (probably all devout Churchillians) who recently threw out the just case of Professor Laski. Remember, too, that in a British court a perfectly true statement may be libellous. So Churchill gets (it's said) $25,000 from Harper Brothers for his sinking treasury and a lot of new prestige in America. One American admirer offered to pay for a gigantic statue of Churchill to be raised on the chalk cliffs of Dover, the nearest point of England to the continent, but the district, though conservative, rejected the idea. It's not in the public interest that such political adventurers should be rewarded as Churchill has been. He deserted the Tory party of his set when power was passing to the Liberals, and he went back to Toryism when he saw power slipping back to the Conservatives. The heads of both parties despised him until the desperate war against the Axis made it necessary to make use again of his vast energy and unquestionable ability. But his blunders (largely from conceit) prolonged the war, and the British public showed its contempt of what is called his "great war reputation" by, at the first opportunity, turning him and his friends down by an immense majority.

❖   ❖   ❖

## "ABIE'S IRISH ROSE" AGAIN

Bing Crosby, who sold his crooked racing racket after making a hit as a young movie priest, has produced a new version of "Abie's Irish Rose," a so-called comedy in which Jews cry "Oy, oy, oy" and the Irish go in for many "bejabbers" both stereotypes that can do nothing but harm. "Abie's Irish Rose" poses as a picture that'll encourage racial harmony, but, instead, the wretched piece of rubbish helps continue misconceptions about the Jews and results in increased prejudice. The old, out-worn stage stereotype of the Jewish people evokes inane laughter, and that laughter leads to the belief that Jews are eccentric, idiotic, ignorant, uncouth, primitive greenhorns. How many Jews talk and gesture the way they're pictured in Bing Crosby's abortion? The so-called Jewish mannerisms were exaggerations two generations ago, and now, with a Jewish population that consists mainly of second and third generation Americans, the caricature is cruel and unjust. Not one Jew in a thousand acts and talks the way Jewish stereotypes are made to ridicule themselves in that appalling piece of trash, "Abie's Irish Rose." The picture poses as a medium for understanding between Jews and Catholics, but in reality it's a device for making the Jews objects of ignorant, boorish, stupid laughter. This picture, presented by one of the Catholic Church's outstanding laymen, will cause pain and hardships to an innocent people who have already suffered too much. "Abie's Irish Rose" will appeal to the sadistic impulses of the ignorant, with "tolerance" as a cloak for the very prejudices it'll provoke. Bing Crosby is using his prestige and capital to increase the sufferings of a helpless minority.

❊ ❊ ❊

## THE POET AND THE SCIENTIST

A new translation of Goethe's "Metamorphosis of Plants," with useful notes by Agnes Arbar, reminds us again that a great poet can't only be a zealous student of science but do important original work in it. Leonardo da Vinci had proved it centuries earlier, and in the Arab-Persian civilization of the Middle Ages many poets—Omar Khayyam, for instance — were 'keen students of science and many men of science wrote poetry. Goethe, the second greatest poet of Europe, is the finest example of a blend of greatness in art and distinction in science. He was so keen in fact that he once said to Eckermann. "I attach no importance to all that I have done as a poet but I'do claim superiority in that I was the only man of my age to learn the true nature of color." It happens that he was wrong in his theory of color, but he made shrewd. observations on the evolution of the eye, and in botany he came near to—in fact he vaguely grasped—the truth of evolution. In geology he made much personal observation and independently discovered the Ice Age in Europe. He, at a time when fossils were believed to be all sorts of odd freaks in stone, recognized them as the remains of extinct races of animals, and in his closing years, when controversy about evolution began, he suported the evolutionists. He held that matter is eternal and rejected all Christian doctrines as well as that of creation. Germans maintain that he founded the science of comparative anatomy. His scientific record is remarkable for the author of "Faust" and requires some explaining by those who, think that the study of science deadens the feeling for art and romance.

❊ ❊ ❊

## TEACHING CITIZENSHIP

A daily opened a short correpondence on the subject matter of teaching in primary and high schools and it elicited a letter from a pupil that is worth reproducing:

As another schoolgirl I agree with your three correspondents who feel that they should be taught something of current affairs. But in order to understand these fully some general background of history is essential: I mean economic or political history, so that the pupil sees how mistakes have been made in the past and learns how to avoid them in the future. Merely learning strings of dates appears to me quite meaningless.

This is an exceptionally thoughtful schoolgirl, of course, but perhaps teachers would find on sympathetic inquiry that the type is not so uncommon. However that may be, the letter strongly confirms the criticisms of the educational system in which we indulge occasionally. We could strike out a vast amount of geographical and historical stuff that's now crammed into the minds of every child. Many feel even that the great majority of folk can get through life without algebra and geometry. In their place, and even suppressing home-work altogether, we could provide elementary lessons in social history and science and economics that would make a beginning of the vital education of youth. Facts about the life they're entering as citizens with democratic rights both appeal more cogently and are less easily forgotten than facts about a remote age or country. They would kindle in large numbers a desire for some attractive form of continuation-classes and provide a foundation for them. We don't lack a sound concept of education today but we do sadly lack consistency in applying it.

✤ ✤ ✤

## ANOTHER NEW JESUS

Robert Graves, a British novelist or writer of history in the form of fiction whose works have had considerable success in this country, has a new and provocative work out with the title "King Jesus." Some reviewers are afraid even to tell their readers why he speaks of Jesus as a king, and his audacity does express some disdain of the writers and speakers who talk about "our Christian civilization" as if all Americans except a few eccentric people still closed their eyes and swallowed the old stories. Graves's idea is that Jesus was a son of Prince Antipater, who was a son of King Herod, and he was therefore the legitimate King of the Jews. Nice to have such an aristocratic origin, but the theory sweeps away all the supposedly vital elements of the Christian story from the Virgin Birth to the Resurrection and Ascension. Of course, the novelist disarms the police by representing that out of this fleshy Herod family is born a prince who lays aside all ideas of political royalty and wants only to be the spiritual king of the race, the leader of the forces of good against the powers of evil. The novel has a much more mystic flavor than the gospels themselves. So we have one more Jesus in the gallery to choose from: Jesus the God on earth, Jesus the great moral genius, Jesus the Essenian monk, Jesus the central figure of an old Jewish pageant play, Jesus the solar myth, and so on. Most of us will decide to get on with the washing and "let the dead bury their dead." Some day, perhaps, the race may have settled its problems and have a little time to spare. At present all this talk about ancient Judea is a distraction, and a particularly unprofitable one in view of the lack of evidence.

✤ ✤ ✤

## THE STIRRING IN LATIN AMERICA

The press has a lot to say about Europe, and the farther away the European country is and the more it's screened by iron curtains the more the press has to say about it. One would have thought that the people of South or Latin America would get more attention, but we hear little more than the fact that representatives of various Latin-American republics are persuaded in one way or other to support us loyally at UN. People are left under the impression that South America still groans under picturesque dictators or, if you prefer it, basks in the sunshine of

16

real Freedom and Private Enterprise. Most people have probably forgotten how after World War I Russian literature was imported by the shipload and there was a remarkable Swing to the Left from the Panama to Patagonia; and how the present Pope then visited all the republics and persuaded the sleek liberal bankers and merchants, the heirs of Bolivar and other great Skeptics, who had fought the "Blacks" for 100 years, that in this spiritual crisis, when every man's bank account and little love-nest are threatened, it's wiser to go to church and form an alliance with the army, the bishops, and the conservatives. It looks as if the Swing to the Right is reversed in many republics. A British Labor lord, Strabolgi, has recently traveled from Mexico to Argentina. His verdict is that "while the United States has been swinging to the Right, Latin America is swinging to the Left." In all the republics from Mexico right down to Cape Horn "the Progressives are not only in the ascendant but are claiming to model their present future policy on the British Labor program." He refers particularly to Mexico, Uruguay, and Chile but finds a strong Leftist movement in the Argentine. Strabolgi is no youthful or advanced optimist but an experienced and careful observer.

❖ ❖ ❖

# FRAUDULENT MEASUREMENTS OF PROGRESS

One of the facts which, it would seem, even the most audacious of sophists cannot dilute away is that the world has grown better in the same proportion as the influence of the churches has diminished. The more ignorant apologist protests that it's "more sinful," in which he betrays how little he has read about manners and morals a century or two ago—probably only a discreet life of Washington and his wife—or says that it's "only in material things" that there has been considerable progress. In the case of Europe, where the old world developed steadily, the real progress is easily measured. One out of many broad facts is that the worker is two or three times as well-off as he was at the beginning of the last century and immensely better treated than in the Middle Ages. A bold sophist has recently contended that this is an illusion: the familiar illusion about the value of money. You say, he argues, that the average wage of the workers in the Middle Ages was about 20c a week, in the early 19th century $2.50 a week, and now at $20 a week, but you don't add that in purchasing value the money-reward of labor was much the same. Bunk. Professor Thorold Rogers has a large and learned work on the status of the workers in Britain—there are others for France and Germany—in the Middle Ages. They worked at least 70 hours a week on 300 days in the year and were housed and fed like pigs. As to the contention that $2.50 a century ago bought as much as $20 today it's moonshine. In England in the early 19th century bread costs nearly as much as it did in 1938 (and was heavily adulterated with cement and ground bone), and the worker bought little else. He had little meat or milk, and no tea, sugar, coffee, cocoa, fruit (except what he stole), eggs, butter, etc. Prices of everything except potatoes and rough fat were beyond him. He is literally three times—if you consider entertainment, transport, etc., five or six times—as well-off. And if the world is wise that gain will be tripled in the present century.

❖ ❖ ❖

# AMERICA AND THE REST OF THE WORLD

American policy in the larger sense underwent so violent a change in the last two years that it reminds us of the old type of religious conversion of boys and girls in their teens. From being mainly isolationist and disdainful of the quarrels of over-sea people it has announced, with as much modesty at it could, that it has taken over the leadership of the race. Many nations applauded vigorously; and by a curious coincidence most of them were deeply indebted, or hoped soon to become indebted, to our country. Many nations said that behind the conversion was an urge analogous to that of the youthful converts to religion: the pressure of a marvelous productive efficiency which called for the lion's share of world-trade. Some malicious nation said that it just meant that the heads of the army and navy, finding themselves for the first time in charge of the greatest armies and navies in the world, had an attack of the "glory" or power-fever that lingers from the Middle Ages. However that may be, it's not working well. Britain, for instance, is the most deeply indebted to this country of all but the obsequiousness of Mr. Bevin mustn't be taken to express the attitude of British people generally. Over more than one-half of Europe sentiment is not friendly. You can't get rid in a year of the effect of 100 years of isolation and contempt. Few of us really understand Europe, and the press reflects its life in a distorting mirror. The wiser guides of the public are working for a readjustment.

❖ ❖ ❖

## IS THE DEVIL JOBLESS?

Among the books published last fall was one with the title "Witchcraft and Black Magic." The author, Montague Summers, has the well-known pages of curious history and the well-known hysterical lies about Satan-worship. It is, therefore, not surprising that he thinks that "the cult of Satan, still enthusiastically recruiting in every land, has enormously increased in the last five years." He seems to think that our age is capable of anything and is tempted to see the hand of the devil in our confusion. But if there's one thing of which our age is incapable it's of ever again taking the devil seriously. He is, it's true, not yet definitely amongst the jobless. He still has his Catholic and Fundamentalist supporters, though he's not now mentioned in sermons or conferences of the intellectually politer sects. The majority in every advanced civilization regard him as an ancient and outworn joke. The last spread of a real cult of Satan was in France in the 17th century, and in Catholic areas, often with priests (not, as is said, apostate priests) and ministers. Isolated neurotic imitations since that time—small groups pretending to have Black Masses, etc.—were just sensual and sensationalist orgies of jaded young men and women who would have fled to church if a devil had shown the tip of his tail. Such isolated orgies were, as is known, held in England (Medmenham Abbey) in the days of Byron, and when that incurable joker, John Wilkes, one night surreptitiously introduced an ape into the room, there was a panic. No, the devil's great days are over. He has now to slink round orthodox chapels pinching the fleshy parts of the worshippers or something of that sort.

❖ ❖ ❖

## DO WE WANT A SUPER-POLITICS?

In some cities there are museums in which we exhibit the vehicles, machines, and technical processes of which our ancestors were so proud: the one-hoss shay, the velocipede, the speaking tube, the tallow candle or oil-lamp, the hand-loom, and so on. We pass through with a smile. We have got leagues beyond all that. Our eyes are ever on the eastern horizon for something new and better. But in two aspects of our national life, one of which is really of basic importance and the other is said to be, we cling to ancient techniques and swear that to depart from them would be violently un-American. The second we call the mechanism for maintaining character at a good social level—religion—the first is the mechanism for promoting our interests as a community, the political machine. Our collective life has developed an extraordinary complexity in comparison with what it was in the days of Jefferson and gives rise to problems that would tax the intelligence of the finest intellects in the nation. But we still rely on the method of sending a few men who either dislike steady work or have glib tongues and a good bedside (or election) manner to get together and see to them. There is, to be sure, a finer civil service at the back of them, but politicians and statesmen can and often do persuade themselves that they know better than the experts of the departments. Representatives of the people there must always be. Thousands of years of history prove the need. But haven't we reached a stage when councils of men of the highest and specific ability are needed to make a profounder study of the national life?

❖ ❖ ❖

## THE CAUSES OF THE REFORMATION

Several historical manuals written by American professors in recent years contain novel ideas about what we call the Reformation or the split of Christendom in the 16th century. The authors smile superciliously at the theory of the "superficial" historians of the last century: that it was inspired entirely or mainly by the appalling corruption of the Roman Church. The latest offender gives the new "scientific" theory as generally accepted in history, which is a monstrous untruth. Back of it, of course, is the pressure of American Catholicism, and no historian who is not exposed to that pressure has any respect for the new thory. It's that political and social changes in the life of Europe entirely or mainly caused the Reformation. The logic of the theory is as strained as the historical statements on which it's based are exaggerated. The few real changes brought about by the increase of the power of kings had litle more bearing upon the furious religious quarrel than sunspots have on the peculiar history of our time. On the other hand, the long and extraordinary corruption of the Papacy and the church, the bearing of which upon a religious quarrel is obvious to a schoolboy, is more solidly established than ever, though numbers of contemporary documents which emphasize it are still not translated Roundly, all but half a dozen Popes (who did not last long) from 1300 to 1667 (50 Popes) were either personally corrupt or too weak or poor in character to check the demoralization of the now wealthy church in every branch. Even the best Catholic history of the period, that of Dr. Ludwig Pastar, admits most of the truth. To say that this longest and deepest corruption of an ecclesiastical authority in the whole history of religion was only a minor cause of the rebellion against it is an insult to our intelligence.

❖ ❖ ❖

## UPS AND DOWNS

William Morris, the famous artist-socialist a n d humanitarian dreamer of the last century, found an easy solution of most of the social problems. In a properly-ordered (Socialist) state, he said, men would have to work only four hours a day, and then would spend their ample leisure cheerfully in enjoying good art and following the advance of science. There was one snag: Who would do the dirty work? He got over it by claiming that no work is dirty unless you insist on regarding it as such. He invented a new type of citizen, the Golden Dustman (in American, garbage man), a shining figure, like the dukes and knights of old, in the social order. We're finding the route to his golden age; whatever theory of the economic state we hold, far longer and rougher than the poet imagined. Not only does every big strike start anxious talk about the spiral of wages and prices but with every advance in education we blur the line of class-distinctions, and it would be ridiculous to suppose that we'll not go a good deal further in the higher education of the children of the mass of the people. It opens the door of opportunity a little wider. "My kids are not going to slave like I did" is a sentiment that will grow steadily. Technical advances will remove much of the difficulty but it remains. Some of us are old enough to remember the sanitary service of not so many years ago. We've seen men on the fringe of cities thigh-deep in the ordure of 50,000 people. We must leave it to the imagination, but we still have salvage-men and garbage-men, and what's more serious, we still have millions of miners, iron workers, builders, etc., who every week see mouth-watering pictures of the life of the rich folk most of whom don't work at all. Men who accuse radicals of dreaming and then say that they can force or induce three-fourths of the nation to accept this as the final and divinely-ordained social order are—well, optimists, if you like.

✤ ✤ ✤

# ARE YOU A CITIZEN OR A PARASITE?

All through the war, or at least from the time when the danger of an Axis victory was over, and the scramble for goods that followed, you heard people right and left saying: "I don't care what they do provided I get the goods and fun I want." If you talked to them you found that they didn't care the toss of a nickel what happened in post-war Europe, hadn't the least comprehension of the need for a balance of trade, and would as soon think of trying to understand the Bretton Woods Agreement and the International Bank as of sitting down to sweat out an understanding of Relativity. Whether the foreign policy pursued by Byrnes was the best for America, whether it was likely to be improved by substituting a fine soldier for an experienced statesman, whether it was true that plutocracy and sectarianism dictated the proceedings of Washington, whether it was concern for ideals or for dollars that inspired the hatred of Russia, whether it was true that we crowned a crusade against Fascism by using the support at UN of brazenly Fascist countries. . . . They didn't even know that the problems existed. They echoed the fiery sentiments of the morning paper about the need to secure democracy in Burma or Bulgaria but they no more ruled their own national life than they made the corn grow on the plains of Kansas. Every one of them knows from the experience of the last 20 years that there's some disease in the national and international life that breaks out periodically in an ugly rash, but they prefer to dodge their own share of the national distress while it lasts and refuse to read any serious discussion of the disease. Apart from the job, therefore, they let their mental life remain so feeble and superficial that they yield to every fallacy and slogan that comes along. These people are parasites on the community as truly as the young idle rich are on its economic vitality. Democracy wants citizens, not parasites.

# THREATENING THE DEAR OLD SERMON

In one of those pale-faced conferences in which ministers of religion nervously discuss how they are to get the majority of people to go to church again it was proposed the other day that one way was to cut down all sermons to not more than five minutes. Most of us feel that to any preacher with a sense of humor, if there are any, the sermon must be rather a good joke. Several hundred men and women sit meekly, like children in a charity school or criminals in the penitentiary chapel, underneath him while he exhorts them to be good and keep the commandments, with special stress on sex. The fact that clerics figure in the lists of sex-offenders more than any other professional men does not seem to matter. We know a case in which a clergyman's wife found him caressing the maid and urged him to practice what he preached. "My business," he said, "is to preach. Yours is to practice what I preach." Of late years he has had the relief of the alternative of spending half an hour denouncing Atheists or Bolsheviks, but in the main the sermon is an exhortation to virtue; and the less dogma the sect or society has the more time the orator has to give to real preaching. It seems that the worm is turning. People want shorter sermons. It may be disappointing to those who always feel that the preacher is denouncing his neighbor's sins, not his own, or the enormities of folk who do not go to church at all; and preachers of the prosperous sects which are run on business lines know that *their* people won't strike. But there it is. There is writing on the sanctuary wall. The dear old 20 to 30 minute sermon is threatened. Hymn-singing and all flattery of the deity may be threatened next.

❖ ❖ ❖

# OUGHT THE CLERGY TO COMMIT SUICIDE?

Many of us swooped with joy and great expectations on an article in an evening paper, written by a clergyman, with the above title. Half the race would probably give a cheerful affirmative to the question. A fine British reformer, George Jacob Holyoake, was sent to jail in the last century for saying in a lecture that it was time we thought of putting the deity on half-pay. But there's no proof that a deity is responsible for these mischievous activities of economic organizations of priests from Japan to Argentina. In the Abolition fight Theodore Parker said that they would make more progress if the churches dropped through the floor of the continent. We should make better progress in every department if it happened today. That's not likely and the alternative is for the clergy to disappear; and since they'd be helpless on the labor and professional markets, euthanasia seems to be desirable. A public subscription to procure means to carry it out painlessly would get a generous response. But, alas, when I read the article I found that the title was a catch. The man's point was that a clergyman's work (which on five days out of seven consists in tea and talk with the more attractive or more generous ladies of the parish) is so exhausting that if one continues to work until he's 60, when he might expect a pension, he commits suicide. The clerical writer feels such that the public don't·realize this. I agree, but when he goes on to suggest that the remedy is for the public to demand far more ministers I fear that his appeal will fall on deaf ears. The public would prefer even the awful risk of a strike of sky-pilots.

❖ ❖ ❖

## BULLS IN CHINA SHOPS

A malicious critic, commenting on the newspapers' explanation that General Marshall's long and devoted efforts to make peace between the Chinese Communists and Chiang Kai-shek were a splendid training for the office of Secretary of State and Heir to the Throne, tosses off the wisecrack that he was really a Bull in a China Shop. That's an unjust reflection on the general's ability. Who's prepared to prove that he ever tried to make peace between them? In fact, is any peace between them possible until one party succeeds in swallowing the other? At the same time it's peculiar that wherever the Anglo-American victors have left soldiers to clear up the mess that they were compelled to make the prolonged disorder does rather remind us of the old saying about a bull in a china shop. Not only is the floor of each country—China, Annam, Burma, Malaya, Indonesia,, Italy, Austria, Poland, Algeria, Syria, Persia, France, Germany, etc.—strewn with ruins but the planes are still flying in most places. The officers might retort that civilians like Robert Murphy, who preceded them, did not do a conspicuously better job; even that UN and the Peace Conference haven't proceeded with perfect smoothness and efficiency. But it's doubtful if the failure of a few badly selected individuals was the real reason why so much administrative power was left to soldies. The truth is that the heads of the defense forces are encroaching too much on politics everywhere. The British Marshal Montgomery was formally asked the other day whether it was true that he had his eye on the political world. He replied at length and warmly, but didn't answer the question. We refuse to consult scientific genius on our problems and prefer to consult men who have learned only how to smash an opposing army when they have a superior armament.

❖ ❖ ❖

## THE HORROR OF DISUNITY

In the course of some of his many recent addresses to the nation— delivered, he carefully explains, not as a churchman but an American— Cardinal Spellman has occasionally dropped the word disunity. Look out for an atom-bomb wrapped up in that pretty word. It rather suggests a new coalition or Holy Alliance. The bankers and industrialists are going presently to demand severe action against disturbers of the economic unity. Cardinal Spellman's church will call for severe action against disturbers of the social unity—by criticizing his church. It's the most brazen of all the slogans. That a unity based upon justice is seriously desirable in the industrial world is obvious, but unity of thought and creed, which in the present state of the world could be effected only by violent repudiation of the fundamental principle of what's called our national heritage, means the introduction of Fascism into America after stamping it out in Japan, Germany and Italy. Freedom of discussion is not only the first freedom for men to choose but it's an indispensable condition of progress. Until the Reformation the finest progress in Europe was in Italy, Portugal, and Spain. Then freedom of discussion was abolished in those lands, and notoriously, the spirit of progress passed to Germany, Holland, England, and France. It's the great dynamic of social progress. And for a church which does more splashing of ink and ethic than all the others put together to demand that it be free to do so and its critics prevented and calls this national unity, is one of the most cynical features of the age.

❖ ❖ ❖

# PROLONGING SENILITY

A leading scientific periodical says: "To prolong senility and the unhappiness usually associated with it would in truth be a vivisection." Vivisection is not, perhaps, the word most of us would choose. We don't want to force any man or woman to remain on the planet when the rickety frame, dull brain, and peevish temper that are so commonly associated with senility make their appearance. And we rather vivisect ourselves than them if we apply methods of extending this pitiful phase of human life from 5 or 10 to 30 or 40 years. The anti-birth control people are right that in time, when the effect of years of swollen birth rate wears off, the community is going to have a much larger percentage of septuagenarians. But it's a mistake to suppose that the extensive research which is now going on in the medical world aims at prolonging senility. The aim is to discover means of putting it back another 10 or 20, and in time more, years, and already considerable progress has been made. Since even the leading defenders of the private enterprise system claim that they can get rid of the danger of over-production this extension of a man's decades of productive activity or service ought to be welcomed by the community as well as by the aged. When you further reflect that we can hardly continue much longer killing off the babies of the poor—it's not too strong an expression—at the rate we do, that an increasing number of men and women who are killing themselves by unwise living from about 40 onward will be educated, and that technical science will enormously improve in enriching production, we get a more cheerful outlook on the future.

❖ ❖ ❖

Mark Twain: "Good breeding consists in concealing how much we think of ourselves and how little we think of the other person."

* * *

Groucho Marx, describing one of his radio scripts: "It doesn't sound like much when you tell it, but on paper it's worse."

* * *

A woman went into a bookstore for something on cooking and home canning and was sold a copy of John Steinbeck's "Cannery Row."

* * *

W. C. Fields: "William Saroyen is the Father Divine of the literary business."

* * *

A Mexico reader tells us that in his district a 12-year-old boy hanged himself on the way from church. He suggests that the kid's guardian angel had strayed into a bit of philandering. We don't know. Some sermons down south are too much even for angels to counteract.

* * *

H. H. Munroe: "The cook was a good cook, as cooks go; and as cooks go she went."

* * *

George Meredith: "Genius does what it must and talent does what it can."

* * *

Sign: "In God We Trust—All Others Pay Cash."

* * *

Lana Turner: "A criminal is a person with predatory impulses who has not sufficient capital to form a corporation."

* * *

The late Mayor Hylan, of New

York: "The police are fully able to meet and compete with all criminals."

* * *

Sign on road near Kansas town: "Slow Down Before You Become a Statistic."

* * *

Lana Turner: "Where all think alike, no one thinks very much."

There once was a lady in Brantage
Of whom the old mayor took advantage.
Said the county surveyor,
"You'll sure have to pay her;
You've altered the line of her frontage."

* * *

Overheard: "The only thing hotter than a Mick on the make is a virgin on the verge."

* * *

We often have a light-hearted fling at the press but we are not ignorant of many of its difficulties even when there is no iron-curtain. Just now many Americans are interested in the semi-Socialist experiments of the British Labor government. How are the people taking it? By mid-October, 1946, the correspondents were confident that the British public were returning to the cult of Churchill. Next week the municipal elections, which are considered a straw for the general election, were held, and labor announced a net gain of 159 seats. "Great Confidence Vote for Labor" said even the Liberal Press. Next day the same papers recorded a Gallup Poll on "Are you satisfied or dissatisfied with the government's record to date?" It appears that their popularity had declined in two months and less than half of the folk who had just voted Labor were satisfied. It is interesting that the government's foreign policy has remarkable support amongst Churchill's followers but has caused an unprecedented rebellion in the party.

* * *

Mr. Jack Benjamin writes us about a paragraph in The Freeman in which, he says, we "strongly" object to a "friendly" criticism in the Truthseeker of Joseph McCabe's "Dictionary of Freethinkers." We have looked up the paragraph, which we find rather playful than strong, and the criticism, which to the naked eye seems rather strong than playful. But Mr. Benjamin still fails to see the point of our complaint, which is that the writer in the Truthseeker got his heavily ironical points only by completely misrepresenting the book. One would think that any man who reads the title alone of the book, "Biographical Dictionary of Ancient, Medieval, and Modern Freethinkers," would know what to expect. The Haldeman-Julius organization has done a great work for American readers in bringing out solid works at a low price but it really can't give you an encyclopedia for 75c. As is plainly stated on the first page of the book, it contains "just a selection," and it could hardly be expected to give the reader a biographical sketch of every second or third-line Freethought speaker of modern times. McCabe considered that the most useful thing he could do in so short a book was to enable Freethinkers to say, in reply to the common opinion that they are a negligible bunch, that large numbers of distinguished or notable men and women were really Freethinkers and to give the full evidence of this, besides a few details (for reference) about such leaders as Voltaire and Ingersoll. The Truthseeker was heavily satirical about the omission of such names as Cohen and Macdonald. In its "friendly" way it did not think fit to add that such men as Bertrand Russell, Haldeman-Julius, Joseph Lewis, and Joseph McCabe himself were omitted. To mention that would have warned the readers at once of the real scope of the books. It is, of course, open to any Freethinker to say that he would like to have biographical sketches of all the men who do Freethought lecturing or writing. That doesn't excuse a reviewer who misrepresents a book with a different object. That sort of thing might be left to the enemy.

Behind it all, of course, there is another quarrel. In fact behind that there is another, for the Truthseeker published years ago a really vicious attack on McCabe by the late Franklin Steiner, without explaining the deplorable scandal in the American Freethought movement which it was meant to cover up. However, the more recent fact is that three years ago an anonymous contributor to the *Truthseeker*, masquerading as an historian ("Historicus"), occupied the front pages, in large type, of that paper with a "friendly" criticism of what he called "recent"—they were, as he knew, 15 years old—criticisms by McCabe of the Jesus-myth theory. Out of courtesy for the serious readers of the paper McCabe sent a succinct statement of his real position (published on a back page in small type). He explained that he is not interested in the four or five contradictory and often fantastic theories of the origin of a myth of Jesus, especially as he considers it broadly probable that there had been an historical Jesus. As the writers found their chief point in the massive authority of the mythicist writers—one of them said that "McCabe ought to know better" and ought to bow to the opinion of "more eminent colleagues"—and they clearly knew nothing about most of them (a cashier, a high school-teacher, a commercial artist, a novelist, and two metaphysicians), and pointed out that, while most historians are reticent for business reasons, he could quote a dozen avowed Rationalist historians of world-repute, all experts on the period, who took the same view as himself, but not one who took the mythicist view. Phew! That threw the fat in the fire, and as the language grew more acrid and his position and argument were persistently misrepresented, McCabe gradually withdrew. Apparently the embers still smolder in New York

\* \* \*

Patsy O'Bang: "Even when Mrs Priscilla Prissy-Pratt walks one feels that she has ants in her panties."

\* \* \*

Jimmy Durante: "Don't raise the bridge, boys, lower the river!"

\* \* \*

Evanston, Ill., has an ordinance prohibiting the changing of clothes in a car with the curtains drawn.

\* \* \*

According to the dairy of Count Ciano, Mussolini's son-in-law, two German officers in January, 1942, forced their way into the home of an Italian who was about to go to bed and said: "We took France, Belgium, Holland and Poland. Tonight we will take your wife." To which the man replied: "You may take the whole world, but not my wife. I am a bachelor."

\* \* \*

Mickey Rooney: "W. C. Fields, Charlie Chaplin and Groucho Marx have a great deal to learn. I wish I had time to teach them."

\* \* \*

Stanislaus: "What is Fame? The advantage of being known by people of whom you yourself know nothing, and for whom you care as little."

\* \* \*

When the late Tom Mix was at the peak of his popularity and he was taking in $17,000 per week, he built an enormous house at the top of a hill in Beverly Hills, and atop the house he put the initials of his name in electric lights.

\* \* \*

Mark Twain: "Principles have no real force except when one is well fed."

\* \* \*

W. C. Fields: "There was a sucker in a mining town who played a crooked wheel in the saloon night in and night out. Tipped off that the wheel was jacked against him, he responded, 'But what can I do? It's the only one in town'."

\* \* \*

Patsy O'Bang: "Waiter, I want coffee without cream." Waiter: "Sorry, can't serve coffee without cream." O'Bang: "Then why have you served coffee without cream to those people over there?" Waiter: "You're wrong. That's coffee without milk. Our cream is all gone."

\* \* \*

Max Beerbohm: "My whole position (as a critic) is unfortunate. When I am laughing at anyone I am generally rather amusing, but when I am praising anyone, I am always deadly dull.'"

\* \* \*

A British medical journal boasted of progress in reducing infant mortality. In 1850 it was 150 to every 1000 births in Britain: in 1944 it was down to 40 per 1000. Whereupon an urban doctor wrote that it was no more than 25 per 1000 among the comfortable classes, but in a city 108 amongst the poor generally and 153 amongst the unemployed poor. A good many folk just now who are worried about population want to bribe mothers to have more children. They ought to know that almost the only parents who would respond to such a bribe as they are likely to offer are the poor. Far better spend the money in supplying nourishment and education to stop the mortality. We have to remember that the deaths mean not only distress to mothers but widespread suffering in a whole class even when the baby pulls through.

* * *

Somebody has revived a story that when Lord Crew, who died recently, was a youth his father took him to see Carlyle. They had just seen Herbert Spencer and told Carlyle. "An unmitigated ass," Carlyle growled. The story is true but incomplete. The fact is that when the father had told Spencer that they were going to see Carlyle he pursed his lips and murmured. "A most mischievous man."

* * *

There is a new slogan in the higher world of philosophy and theology. The respective spheres of science and religion are now definitely marked and there is to be no more skirmishing. Science deals with caused events, religion with things that are done for a purpose. As all these superior folk have taken up the cry that events in the world of electrons are not caused, do they propose to hand that over to our doctors of divinity? And if events in the sphere of psychology and economics are not things done with a purpose what is purpose? The theologians must try again. They have plenty of leisure.

* * *

One of the scores of Americans who have flown the ocean in the last month or two to see how these British really live has found that their education is "waste-ridden and money-dominated." So very different from the American system.

* * *

Mr. and Mrs. New Rich were entertaining. "Do you like Botticelli?" the guest on her right mischievous-ly asked the lady. "Yes," she said, "but I prefer Chianti". When the guests had gone the husband said to her. "Try not to make a ruddy fool of yourself, Sadie. Botticelli isn't a wine. It's a cheese."

* * *

Bishop Beerbelch: "I know that Materialists like Haldeman-Julius will call this argument bowelpaste, but I still insist it gives positive proof of God's position as the universe's architect. I refer to the demonstrated fact that cork trees grow mainly in the countries that are great producers of wine, particularly Portugal and Spain. Think of His divine thoughtfulness in placing the corks in such a handy place so that wine-growers may have little trouble in getting their fluids bottled. The Benedictine monks discovered this interesting fact. As all drinkers of fine likker know, these monks turn out a much-appreciated article that travels in bottles to all parts of the world. They don't have to go far for their corks. God has taken care of that problem for them."

* * *

A big authority on tropical diseases, Director of the Ross Institute, has publicly stated that these diseases are now so far under control that the tropics will soon be as healthy to live in as the United states. That opens up a remarkable prospect for Africa and South America.

* * *

A distinguished novelist telephoned urgently for the family physician. His young son had, he said, swallowed his fountain pen. "Coming right over" said the doctor. "What are you doing in the meantime?" "Oh, I'm carrying on as well as I can with an ordinary pen."

* * *

An old lady died the other day leaving an estate of about $20,000 to be divided amongst a large group. The will stipulated that any beneficiary who left the church, was immoral, or caused unpleasantness in any way whatever was to be disinherited It was taken to court and the judge told them to tear up the will. The woman, he said, "could not be allowed to rule the world from her grave." Good. We shall next discover that there are people who have been ruling the world from their graves for the last 1900 years.

* * *

While in Kansas City, Clarence Darrow was visited by a committee that wanted to know what he'd charge for a lecture. "My fee," said Darrow, "is $150 if I select the subject and $250 if the committee selects the subject—and in either case you get the same speech."

* * *

John Barrymore, to secretary who announced Louis B. Mayer on the phone: "I'll take the call, but first clear off my table so I can pound on it."

* * *

Oscar Wilde: "I must decline your invitation owing to a subsequent invitation." . . . "Duty is what we expect from others." . . . "Humanity takes itself too seriously—that is the original sin." . . . "Reform in dress is much more important than reform in religion." . . . "Nothing succeeds like excess." . . . "I was working on the proof of one of my poems all the morning and took out a comma. In the afternoon I put it back." . . . To U. S. customs official who asked if he had anything to declare: "Only my genius." . . . "In America life is one long expectoration." . . . "The habit in America of hanging pictures up near the cornice struck me as irrational at first. It was not until I saw how bad the pictures were that I realized the advantage of the custom." . . . On receiving a wire from Griggsville, "Will you lecture us on esthetics?" Wilde replied: "Begin my changing the name of your town." . . . "Never put off till tomorrow what you can do the day after." . . . "Give me the luxuries and I can dispense with the necessities." . . . "Missionaries are the divinely provided food for destitute and underfed cannibals. Whenever cannibals are on the brink of starvation, Heaven in its infinite mercy sends them a nice plump missionary." . . . "The proper basis for marriage is a mutual misunderstanding." . . . "She who hesitates is won."

* * *

When Bishop Beerbelch died and went to heaven, he was taken on a sight-seeing tour, during which he came on Priscilla Prissy-Pratt and an old-maid aunt of hers. The two women were behaving oddly. Priscilla would give her aunt a stiff kick, after which the aunt would give Priscilla Prissy-Pratt an equally stiff kick in return. This continued hour after hour, and had been going on for a long time. Curious, Bishop Beerbelch turned to his guide and asked: "Why are those two women kicking each other?" "Oh," replied the angel, "they've been doing that ever since they learned that one doesn't have to be a virgin to get into heaven."

* * *

From a help wanted ad: "Experience essential but not necessary."

* * *

While passing through the Ozark country recently I was impressed by the way marriages stay put down in those mountains. As my survey was superficial, I can only say that here is a theme for careful inquiry, for there's no excuse for a hasty generalization, but from my surface view I'm moved by the spectacle of mountain men never getting tired of mountain women. Why this is so, I don't know. Maybe some informed reader can give me the exact dope.

* * *

The Army lost a great leader when Patsy O'Bang decided to turn to the 40 sciences. In uniform, he devoted himself wholeheartedly to the problems of tactics and strategy. Ever the disciplinarian, Lieut. Patsy O'Bang growled to a corporal: ::What's this I hear about your being so drunk last night that you pushed a wheelbarrow through every one of the native huts? Is that the way to keep face with these Filipinos?" "You ought to know, Lieut. O'Bang," answered the corporal. "You were in the wheelbarrow."

* * *

Dr. Patsy O'Bang, world's greatest biologist and anthropologist: "Man is a cornivorous animal."

* * *

Simon and Schuster plan to publish a book called "Lady Loverley's Chatter."

* * *

Pat came home from a wild party. It was late, and he slipped into the room as quietly as he could, thinking that Bridget was asleep. But

Bridget wasn't, and as he undressed she could see by the electric signs outside that he had come home without his underwear. "Pat!" she cried out "where are your shorts?"—and she turned on the light. Pat looked down at himself in blank astonishment for a moment. "Police!" he shouted at the top of his voice. "I've been robbed!"

* * *

I've already told about that peculiar name for a brand of baking powder, "Clabber Girl." Yesterday, near Joplin, Mo., I came on this one, "Darling Fertilizer."

* * *

Sir Thomas Beecham: "Women in an orchestra tend to distract the more inflammable male members. If the woman happens to look like Mrs. Priscilla Prissy-Pratt, he doesn't want to play next to the battle-axe; if she is well-favored, he can't."

* * *

Groucho Marx: "The last time I made a trip around the world I came home with a poor opinion of it."

* * *

Groucho Marx: "Clever liars give details, but the cleverest don't."

Samuel Butler: "All progress is based upon a universal innate desire on the part of every organism to live beyond its income."

* *

Mother, watching her daughter dressing for the evening: "Betty, you're not wearing panties!" "No, I'm not." "But don't you think you should?" To which protest Betty responded: "Mother, if you were expecting to be kissed would you wear a veil?"

* * *

There is a new book out on *The Philosophy of Jesus*. Doubtless this new and more powerful X-ray apparatus has been used to make a more thorough search.

* * *

J. B. S. Haldane: "The only people who are professionally concerned with eternity are clergymen and astronomers." . . . "The clergy have a vested interest in ignorance." Haldane's description of eternity: "Imagine a mountain of steel. Every century a bird comes and drops a feather on it. When the mountain is worn away, a soul in torment asks what is the date, and is told 'eternity has just begun'."

* * *

Press item that should be checked: "The surface of Russia is the size of the moon."

* * *

Sign in restaurant: "Don't take the silver after meals—it ain't medicine."

* * *

Rooster: "Patience is a great thing but it'll never help me lay an egg."

* * *

Drew Pearson's column says the battleship Missouri "was rushed to Istanbul and it was made quite clear that the U.S. was on the side of peace." Say it with flowers, battleships and A-bombs.

* * *

For years, consumers have been working for a simple, reasonable grade labeling law in order to know what canned goods contain. Thus far, we consumers have been thoroughly screwed by the canning companies. For example, buying a can of tomatoes or tomato juice is like shooting craps with a professional—the consumer always loses. It's been years since I've had either, because I could tell after the first taste that I'd been paying high prices for water. An honest can of tomatoes is a rarity. Only a federal law could control such a situation, and yet it's been impossible thus far to get such a law. The arguments against the law often are amusing because the canning interests can't get around the obvious fact that there really are no arguments against it—from the viewpoint of the consumers. Spokesmen for the food industry fight the drive with appeals to Americanism, patriotism, anti-Communism, Free Enterprise. the defense of pure womanhood, and the sinfulness of questioning the only people who really love Old Glory. Here's how Henry E. Abt, managing director of the Brand Names Research Foundation, let loose: "Compulsory grade labeling, frequently advocated by the government, would betray the consumer's confidence by eliminating the producer's responsibility to maintain high-quality standards."

* * *

Oscar Levant, the Dead End Kid

of Music, never hesitates to insult bores. After one of his concerts, he was taken in charge by a famous conductor, who complained: "You don't know how to bow. You must learn to bow." Oscar gave him a withering look and blurted: "You bow beautifully. I'd rather see you bow than hear you conduct."

* * *

No, sir! It wasn't Robert G. Ingersoll who first asked the question. "Why doesn't God kill the devil?" The Red Indians of Massachusetts stumped missionary John Eliot with that poser 300 years ago. "Why does not God, who has full power," inquired those naive savages, "kill ye devil, that makes all men bad?"

Bishop Beerbelch had just finished with the wedding ceremony when the groom, a plumber, said to him in a whisper: "Sorry, Bishop Beerbelch, I haven't any money, but I can stop your gas meter from registering."

* * *

Many papers, much to their credit, try to interest the public in a new astronomical theory. It sets out to explain the spiral form or "spin" of the hundreds of thousands of separate universes which are disclosed on photographs of the heavens. If the theory is sound, these papers point out, we have every reason to suppose that it is common, if not the usual thing, for a star to have a retinue of planets. We admire these efforts to lift the minds of readers occasionally above baseball, politics, and the small size of steaks. But have not the editors forgotten that 20 years ago they gave the same or a greater prominence to the theory of Sir James Jeans that the possession of a family of planets by our sun must be an extremely rare, if not unique, phenomenon in the universe? It gave great comfort to the churches. A claim has lately been made and is being seriously considered that photographs show large planets attending some of the nearer stars.

* * *

The recent eclipse of the sun had some curious effects. Even when it was only partial the excitement was great. In a Scottish prison the whole staff caught the fever and glued its eyes on the spectacle. When it was over they found that several of the prisoners had climbed the wall and disappeared.

* * *

"Why didn't you zig-zag your car and avoid the man?" a coroner asked a chauffeur who had run down an intoxicated man. "I did," he said, "but the man was zig-zagging himself and ran into me."

* * *

A medical journal begins an article on the dear old topic of juvenile delinquency with this sentence: "Much is heard in these days about juvenile delinquency but the problems of the aged delinquent tend to be forgotten." It gives statistics to prove that there is a problem. Now we shall have to begin all over again reading how the films debauch these old folk, how they must be put under compulsory religious instruction, how sons and daughters, who ought to keep an eye on them, are in the beerhouses, and all the rest of it. Someone will probably organize a Legion of Youth to keep the old folk in order.

* * *

American officers in London rubbed their eyes when, the other day, they opened the *Times* and read this advertisement: 'Wanted, an electric chair in good condition."

* * *

When the medical authorities began to immunize against diphtheria it was cynically said that it meant new jobs. From 1910 to 1920 the cases of diphtheria in New York averaged 14,282 a year and the deaths 1,270. It is claimed that the annual number of cases has fallen below 5000 and the deaths to about 10, and it costs 50 times more to treat a case than to immunize.

* * *

One of the latest books to appear in the religious book-stores, on which we keep an eager eye, is *Is Modern Culture Doomed?* It explains, with a certain lack of originality, that scientific materialism has debauched and is ruining the world. It summons the world to cast off the nightmare and return to "the radiant joy and deep contentment of the life inspired by faith."' It is amazing how such blah still finds readers. The Countries which scientific materialism has not yet affected are amongst the most diseased and poverty-stricken on earth and are neither joyous nor virtuous. This sort of literary business thrives on lies about the Middle Ages and our historians are now afraid to tell the truth.

* * *

A visitor took a few bananas to a children's hospital in England. Several of the youngsters had never seen one before, or did not remember them, and they refused to touch them. They were un-English.

* * *

Many will remember the wrestler Hackenschmidt "the world's strongest man." He has set up as a philosopher and is about to publish a book on cosmic problems. Muscling in, so to speak. But philosophy can do with a little more blood.

* * *

"The difference between matter and spirit" says the latest spiritual oracle, "is of a purely electronic nature." So now we know. We have been asking these folk for 20 years to tell us what they mean by spirit. But if matter consists of electrons and spirit also consists of electrons why all the fuss about materialism? And how light-heartedly this expert throws over all the authorities on spirit from Plato to the present Pope. They were all quite clear that by spirit they meant something timeless and spaceless.

* * *

"Really," said Mrs. Scott, reading her paper at breakfast, "the world is getting worse and worse. Just listen to this advertisement. "Typist wanted, must be young, fast, and experienced."

* * *

A new book is out with the title *From Microbe to Man*. The title has already been used several times for manuals of evolution, but this is really different. It closes with the singular conclusion that if we will return to religion the millennium will open.

* * *

There is such a fine public just now for discoveries of secrets of nature that someone has revived one of Marconi's. He was told of a flock of migrating storks which swooped down on a lake that proved to be full of frogs. The frogs were not visible to the human eye, and they had taken to the water long before the storks could be seen. Marconi said that all animals—including man before he began to wear boots—have a sort of radio receiving set in their feet. Marconi certainly knew a lot about radio but not about the foot. But that doesn't matter today. The one thing needful is to be able to see through a brickwall—or say so.

* * *

A clergyman brought as a witness in a juvenile court the other day had a long conversation on juvenile crime with the sympathetic judge. All due to lack of religious instruction, of course. Teachers, the parson said, were relying on "the pragmatic ethics of today." That stumped the judge, and the parson blandly explained that pragmatic meant judging things by results. His dislike of such a procedure as that was natural. If the Countries in which the schools are drenched with religious instruction were to have this tested by results, or by the statistics of either juvenile or adult crime, it would be very bad for the parson's business.

* * *

A scientific man had finished his lecture on recent progress in physics and was answering questions. "What's the good of it?" one man asked. "What's the good of a baby?" the lecturer retorted.

* * *

An American journalist out in the Near East was trying to penetrate the mystery of the oriental mind. He asked a Moslem what he thought about the American idea of restricting a husband to one wife. "Christian men lazy," said the Syrian.

* * *

One day in November, 1946, we saw two short paragraphs in one column of a metropolitan paper. One ran:

"The American Conference of Christians and Jews has proposed that the United Nations conduct an inquiry into the prosecution of Archbishop Stepniak."

The other said:

"America has sent sharp note to Poland demanding equal rights for Opposition parties in the Polish elections on January 19."

On other pages there were references to the joint Anglo-American rebuff to Rumania and their action in Palestine, Greece, China, Italy, etc. And on another page was an article with this heading in half-inch type:

"Our Set-up in Gemany Is Grossly Inefficient."

How many folk saw the irony? Obviously the editor didn't.

❖ ❖ ❖

That amiable new tactic invented by the Knights of Columbus of paying papers to insert your copy instead of asking payment for it—and some folk call ours a sordidly commercial age—is having its patent infringed. We get a copy of an unnamed Chicago paper in which the Rev. Dallas F. Gorillington—sorry, Billington, but see photo—has a column for the Baptists. "Send sound Baptists to Washington and we will see building permits issued to churches not beer gardens" and other improvements. The text of the sermon (four inches of it) is from Daniel. We shouldn't have thought that Chicago people were likely to be moved by that ancient forgery.

❖ ❖ ❖

Frances Baird writes me to say that a statement in one of my publications that when the Jesuits sought permission to found a society "they were successful largely because of the looseness of their moral guides" is "a deliberate lie." She spells the last word in heroic capitals which makes me blush. But she adduces only the fact that "my brothers were educated by the Jesuits, and I know the principals (?) instilled into them." I take it that this education was not in the 1th century and so does not seem to throw much light on it. In short, any history of the Jesuits not written by a Jesuit will tell the lady that Ignatius of Loyola only got permission to found a society, which was at first sternly refused,

by intrigue and deceit, and that it practiced deceit on an amazing scale until the Pope suppressed it, on that and other moral grounds, in 1773.

❖ ❖ ❖

The British military authorities recognize a category which they call "the semi-illiterate." They report that these were 22 percent of the men taken into the army this year. Somebody ought to demand the recognition of the demi-semi-illiterates and then tell us how many are left. But politicians don't like these finicky distinctions amongst their supporters.

❖ ❖ ❖

Pundit Nehru has said in an important public speech that "free India will have a full Republic in which there will be no rule by the Maharajahs and Nawabs." Every good American will approve, but Nehru went on to say that the Constitution will be "of a Socialistic pattern." Don't be alarmed. The Congress is under the control of rich Hindu and Moslem capitalists. The only Socialists in India are in the Radical Democratic Party, under the brilliant leadership of that great scholar, Mr. Roy.

❖ ❖ ❖

It is said that now that news travels round the earth at 100,000 miles a second everybody knows how everybody else lives and thinks. Here is how it works—sometimes. In the New Zealand *Rationalist,* for September, 1946, there was a quotation from the local Catholic *Zealandia,* for August. This in turn had quoted the Papal newspaper the *Osservatore Romano,* presumably for July and June. So five months after the event, and during all these months the American Catholic press was thundering that the Vatican never interfered in politics, we got this defiant semi-official papal declaration:

"Are these merely temporal affairs? Is it a question of religion and Christian civilization or is it not—this choice between belief in a personal God, with the spiritual dignity and eternal destiny of man and the surrender to an

,o m n i p o t e n t materialistic state without religion?"

The Pope may be consoled to know that the moralists of Wall Street emphatically agree with him. It's all right provided you don't mention Russia in more than a whisper.

❖　❖　❖

An Irish farmer sending his apples to Dublin neatly inserted in one of them a slip of paper with the message: "I sold this apple for a penny. How much did you pay for it?" He got a reply in the course of time from a Dublin woman. She had paid 18c for it. But don't misunderstand. An Irish or British penny is 2c.

❖　❖　❖

How many notice the cry of the press in regard to the recent French elections for the Senate? Before the day of election we were warned on all sides that the French were tired of voting and the result might not mean much. The fact was that owing to de Gaulle's tactless talk a further gain by the Communists was feared. On Monday there was a big front-page announcement that the hybrid Catholic M.R.P. was winning. Then Corsica sent its results, 37,948 votes for Communists and only 588 for Catholics. So on a back-page we learned that the Communists, who had less than a million members in France before the war—the papers didn't remind you of this, of course— got the biggest vote. It's a nuisance. It spoils the symmetry of the formula that Western Europe, being far away from Russia, rejects these Red ideas, and only Russia-dominated Eastern Europe pretends to accept them.

❖　❖　❖

The European elections of 1946 are worth tons of the stuff that "our foreign correspondent" sends in—if he's to keep his job. Allowing for the influence of the occupying power in each region, whether it's Russia or one of the Democracies, They've shown a decided swing to the Left. Early in the year practically all the foreign correspondents said that the swing to the Left of 1945 had become a swing to the Right. Why did they anticipate this? Apart from financial dependence on the Allies and UNRRA, there was a new factor about which they're now silent. *In most of these elections women voted for the first time in history.* In the light of that fact the results are astounding. There's much rubbing of eyes in Vatican City.

❖　❖　❖

One or two of my readers seem to have the illusion that I always criticize Whites and Blacks, never Reds. I have, on the contrary, said repeatedly that to the outsider like myself the feud between the Socialist and Communist shades of Red is folly. The concrete aim of both is the same: nationalization of industry. I'm quite aware that there's a serious background of history to it, but in France, if not generally, it's mainly a quarrel of leaders, as in our Unionism.

❖　❖　❖

Two scientists were lately in a plane crossing the vast region of the Amazon where the jungle is so dense and fed by such steaming heat and downpours that no animal of any size can live in it. It covers 4,500,000 square miles of miraculous fertility and is more useless to the race than the Gobi Desert. "There," said one of the scientific gents, "is the great development-area of the future—the Klondike of the Cellulose Age." There's ground to believe that there's also great mineral wealth underneath that mighty green pall. It's monstrous to leave such regions of the earth under a lazy, greedy, selfish lot like the ruling class at Rio. Some big international scheme could, without disturbing the rights of the Brazilian people, use it to add enormously to the earth's resources. Why not drop our atom bombs on it to begin with?

❖　❖　❖

Old lady: "My constipation is gettin' worse, but I take it philosophic like. All I do for it is to take my knitting."

*　*　*

Groucho Marx, to woman: "With your tongue and a loaf of pumpernickel we could open a delicatessen."

CPSIA information can be obtained
at www.ICGtesting.com
Printed in the USA
BVHW060337120123
656153BV00023B/278